Created by Eugeniya Popova and Lilu Rami
Illustrated by Anastasiya Druzhininskaya

LOOK & FIND

HALLOWEEN HUNT

CLEVER
·Publishing·

Find all the pumpkins with a red bow!

Find the kitten hiding behind a pumpkin.

Find the pumpkin wearing pajamas.

Which pumpkin looks like a musical instrument?

Find the smallest pumpkin.

Which pumpkins have candles in them?

Who has the biggest hat?

Oh no! Her shoe is missing. Can you find it?

Find two identical witches.

Two witches can't share a hat.
Help them find another one.

Which fairy has the most
flowers in her hair?

Find the witch who is
friends with owls.

Find the kid in a pumpkin costume.

Find two of the same costume.

Who is going swimming?

Find the one who came without a costume.

Find five frogs.

Find the witch's broom.

Find the boy in the pirate costume.

Who is eating a banana?

Which two kids have
matching costumes?

Find the knight and the princess.

Who forgot to wear a costume?

Who is wearing a flower costume?

Find the skeleton with headphones.

Who has a magnifying glass?

Who has a bat on their head?

Which skeleton is running?

Find the dark gray mouse.

Which little skeleton is sleepy?

Find the ghost eating a doughnut.

Point to the smallest ghost.

Which ghost is wearing different socks?

Which ghost has an old, patchwork costume?

Can you find the ghost who's scared of a spider?

Find all the ghosts with glasses.

Which basket has the most candy?

Find the cupcake with a witch's hat.

Find five chocolate bars.

Find all the lollipops.

Find the cupcake with bones on it.

Find all the candy spiders.

Find a dog
in a ghost costume.

Find a cat in a
pumpkin costume.

Find all the puppies
in bunny costumes.

Who has the biggest hat?

Find five animals in costumes in the form of food.

Who is a frog?

Who has the longest legs?

Who wears a witch's hat?

Which spider wears glasses?

Find all the chocolate chip cookies.

Which mouse is a pirate?

Find a toy mouse.

Find a cat with flowers on their head.

Find all the green yarn balls.

Find a cat wearing wings.